LITTLE

Planets

James Muirden

Kingfisher Books

Contents

A planet family

Earth is our own planet. It is one of a family of nine planets whirling around the Sun, our star. Together they make the solar system.

The solar system formed thousands of millions of years ago. Before that, there was just a huge dark cloud of gas and dust in space.

In the beginning

O ur Sun and the planets were born from the space cloud about 4,600 million years ago.

First the cloud began to shrink and spin, as its gravity pulled the gas and dust inwards. Then the cloud's centre became very hot and started to glow. This became the Sun. The rest of the gas and dust slowly clumped together to make the planets.

WHAT IS GRAVITY?

Gravity is a pulling force. The Earth's gravity pulls things to the ground, stopping them flying off into space. The Sun's gravity keeps the planets whirling around it.

The first person to understand gravity was Sir Isaac Newton, in 1665. He is supposed to have had a brain wave while watching an apple fall from a tree!

BIRTH OF THE PLANETS

① The Sun formed at the centre, where the space cloud was hottest.

② The Sun's gravity kept some of the gas and dust whizzing around it. The specks of dust clumped together, getting bigger and bigger.

③ The clumps kept on colliding and getting bigger until they formed the nine planets.

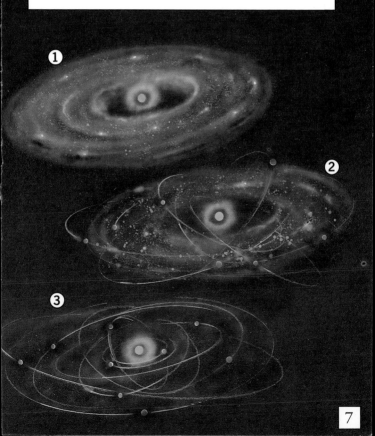

The solar system

All the planets move around the Sun, in an oval path we call an orbit. A planet's year is the time it takes to make one orbit of the Sun.

The Sun shines on the planets, giving them light and warmth. Those closest to the Sun are warmer and go round more quickly.

1. Sun
2. Mercury
3. Venus
4. Earth
5. Mars
6. Jupiter
7. Saturn
8. Uranus
9. Neptune
10. Pluto

PLANET FACTS

Name of planet	Size (x Earth)	Million km from Sun	Year (in Earth time)
Mercury	0.4	58	88 days
Venus	0.9	108	225 days
Earth	1	150	365 days
Mars	0.5	228	687 days
Jupiter	11	778	11.7 years
Saturn	9.4	1,427	29.5 years
Uranus	4	2,870	84.0 years
Neptune	3.8	4,497	164.8 years
Pluto	0.2	5,900	248.5 years

Imagine cutting Earth in half all the way through its middle, and measuring across its widest point – that distance is its diameter. Earth's diameter is 12,756 kilometres. The biggest diameter is Jupiter's, at 142,800 kilometres.

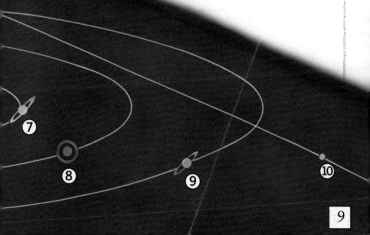

Large and small

Earth seems huge to us, but some of the other planets are much larger still. The biggest is Jupiter. It is so enormous that about 1,300 Earths could be squeezed inside it. Saturn, Uranus and Neptune are also much larger than our planet.

Venus is nearly the same size as Earth, but Mercury, Mars and Pluto are all much smaller. Pluto is tiny – it isn't even as big as our Moon.

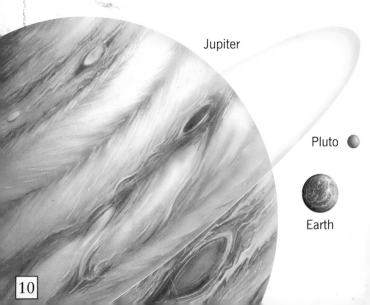

Jupiter

Pluto

Earth

MAKE YOUR OWN SOLAR SYSTEM

It's hard to picture just how big the Sun is in comparison to the planets. One way is to build a mini-solar system – you'll find all the things you need around the house.

Sun	Football (22 cm across)
Mercury	Small plant seed (just under 1 mm)
Venus	Round rice grain (just over 2 mm)
Earth	Round rice grain (just over 2 mm)
Mars	Small pinhead (just over 1 mm)
Jupiter	Walnut (26 mm)
Saturn	Large marble (22 mm)
Uranus	Pea (9 mm)
Neptune	Pea (9 mm)
Pluto	Grain of sugar (less than 0.5 mm)

To get an idea of distances, your rice-grain Earth should be about 25 metres away from the football Sun!

Rocky planets

T he four planets nearest to the Sun
are made mainly of rock. They are
Mercury, Venus, Earth and Mars.

A planet's outer layer is called its
crust. The mantle lies below. Its core is
the middle. This is what the rocky
planets look like inside.

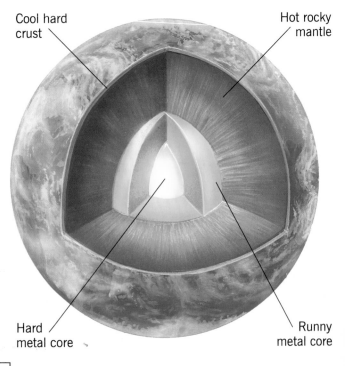

Cool hard
crust

Hot rocky
mantle

Hard
metal core

Runny
metal core

Mercury

Mercury's crust is pitted with craters – hollows made by huge space rocks slamming into it. The planet has no air or water. It is the nearest to the Sun, and by day its dry rocky surface is hotter than an oven. At night, though, it is even colder than Earth's icy north and south poles.

Mercury's craters formed about 4,000 million years ago, when space rocks crashed into it and exploded.

Venus

Even though it isn't the closest to the Sun, Venus is the hottest of the planets. Unlike Mercury, it is covered with thick yellow clouds, which act like a blanket holding in the Sun's heat. Venus's surface can reach 500 °C – hot enough to bake clay pots.

Venus is gloomy even by day, with lightning flickering through the foggy twilight. It once had live volcanoes sending out lava.

Mars

This planet has hardly any air, and its surface is a bitterly cold desert, where the temperature drops as low as –120 °C. Mars is often called the red planet. The ground is covered in rocks and dusty red soil, which gets swept up by the wind to make the sky pink.

In 1976 the USA sent two Viking space probes to Mars. The probes tested the soil for signs of life, but they didn't find anything.

Our living planet

As far as we know, our planet is the only one in the solar system with living things on it. This is because plants, animals and all other living things need water, and Earth is just the right distance from the Sun to have water on its surface. Much closer and the water would boil and vanish into the air. Much farther away, and it would freeze into solid ice.

IS THERE LIFE ON OTHER PLANETS?

There are probably thousands of millions of other solar systems in the universe, but they are too far away for scientists to find out much about them. There may be planets like Earth in some of these solar systems, ones that have living creatures on them.

The star Beta Pictoris is about 800 million million kilometres away from Earth. It has a cloud of gas and dust around it where new planets may be forming.

If there are other planets with life on them somewhere in our part of the universe, the creatures that live there may be sending out radio signals into space. Some scientists are using radio telescopes to try to pick up these signals from space.

We use radio telescopes like this to listen for radio signals from space. These telescopes are different from the ones we use to look at space objects.

Icy giants

The four largest planets in the solar system are made mostly of hydrogen. The 'surfaces' that we see through telescopes are the tops of swirling, freezing clouds. Anyone trying to land on them would just sink into a thick fog of deadly gases.

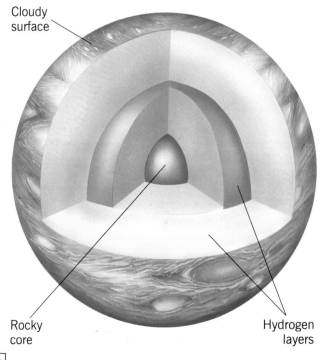

Cloudy surface

Rocky core

Hydrogen layers

Jupiter

The planets are spinning round as they orbit the Sun. A planet's day is the time it takes to spin round once. Jupiter is the largest planet, but it

Great Red Spot

spins the fastest and so has the shortest day – sunrise to sunset on Jupiter is less than five Earth hours long.

Beautifully coloured clouds cover Jupiter's surface, and are pulled into streaks and swirls as it spins. Its Great Red Spot is a gigantic whirlwind – two Earths could fit inside it!

Saturn

The planet Saturn is slightly smaller than Jupiter, and its markings are much fainter. Saturn is most famous for its glistening rings. These are ten times wider overall than the diameter of the Earth.

Uranus

This planet was discovered in 1781. It has lots of narrow rings in orbit around it, and its bluey colour comes from one of its gases, methane.

Neptune

This is the outermost giant planet. It is similar to the planet Uranus, but a bit smaller, and it was discovered in 1846.

THE FARTHEST PLANET

Pluto is usually the most distant planet. But every 248 years, its orbit brings it closer to the Sun than Neptune. This is happening now, and will last until 1999.

Pluto

Sun — Uranus

Neptune

Pluto

Pluto is the smallest planet, and at −240 °C the coldest. It has a moon called Charon, which is almost half its size. Scientists think that both Pluto and Charon are made of ice and rock.

The three outer planets are so far away that it is hard to see them clearly from Earth, even if we look through powerful telescopes. Not a lot was known about any of them until the USA's space probe Voyager 2 reached Uranus and sent back radio pictures during 1986.

Rings and moons

The four icy giant planets all have rings. They are made of millions of orbiting pieces of rock, dust and ice. Saturn's bright wide rings are shown in the picture below. The other planets' rings are very faint.

◁ Pictures taken by space probes show us that Saturn's rings look like this when seen close up. The largest pieces of rock are probably the size of a bus!

Moons

Moons are rocky bodies that orbit planets, and most planets have at least one of them. Some of the planets' moons are larger than Earth's, but others are

Ganymede

much smaller – only a few kilometres across. Like the planet Mercury, most moons are covered in craters.

Jupiter has 16 moons, and the biggest one, Ganymede, is the largest in the solar system. It measures 5,262 kilometres across its diameter.

MOON AND RING FACTS		
Planet	Moons	Rings
Mercury	0	0
Venus	0	0
Earth	1	0
Mars	2	0
Jupiter	16	3
Saturn	18	7
Uranus	15	13
Neptune	8	4
Pluto	1	0

Earth's moon

Our Moon is the closest space body to us in the solar system – only 384,000 kilometres away. It wouldn't take long for a space rocket to travel this distance. But even if we could build a road stretching all the way there, it would still take us more than five months to drive as far as the Moon, travelling day and night at a speed of 100 kilometres an hour.

The Moon's surface is very dusty. There's no water to drink, or air to breathe, and it's boiling hot in the daytime and freezing cold at night.

LOOKING AT THE MOON

The Moon is close enough to the Earth for you to see lots of interesting things just with a pair of binoculars. Choose a bright clear night, and rest the binoculars on something firm to stop them from shaking.

Lava sea

Crater

The lumpy circles are craters. They look small from Earth, but some of them are so big that they could hold several cities as large as London.

The smooth patches are lava deserts which we call seas. The lava flowed out of cracks in the Moon's crust about 3,000 million years ago.

Mini-planets

Asteroids are mini-planets, leftover pieces from when the nine planets formed. There are millions of them in the solar system, orbiting the Sun in a belt between Mars and Jupiter. Most are up to 1 kilometre across, but the largest is 1,000 kilometres in diameter.

The US space probe Galileo gave us a close-up picture of this asteroid in 1991. It is called Gaspra, and it measures about 17 kilometres from end to end. It may have broken off a larger asteroid, in a collision which happened about 200 million years ago.

LOOK FOR A SHOOTING STAR

The tiniest space bodies of all are the size of a piece of sand or gravel. They are called meteoroids, and if one flies into the air around the Earth it burns up as a streak of light – a meteor or shooting star.

The best time and place to look for a meteor is on a dark night, out in the countryside away from the city lights. Wrap up warmly and spend half an hour just gazing at the stars. With luck, you will see at least one or two meteors.

Looking at planets

The best way to discover which planets you are likely to see in the night sky, and where they are, is to look in a newspaper that publishes a monthly night-sky column.

You won't find the planets on an ordinary star map, because they are always on the move and so cannot be marked. Stars can be shown because the star patterns don't change.

Mercury is usually hard to see, but Venus, Mars, Jupiter and Saturn are all bright, and easily seen without a telescope – if you know where to look.

To find the planet Venus, look for a dazzling light, brighter than the stars, in the East before sunrise, or in the West after sunset.

BE A PLANET DETECTIVE

Here are colour clues to help you find some planets. Mars is reddish, Jupiter is white and usually brighter than any star, and Saturn is dimmer and yellowish.

When you think you've identified a suspect, map its position among the nearby stars. Look again a week or two later – if it has moved, it's probably a planet. Saturn may take longer to find, as it moves slowly and is more difficult to tell from the stars.

With binoculars, you may be able to see Jupiter's four largest moons – they look like specks of light very close to the planet.

Index